29548

WITHDRAWN

PUBLIC LIBRARY
Manchester, Iowa 52057

—————•—————

Keep your card in this pocket.

—————•—————

Time Kept --
 Books may be kept two weeks and may
be renewed once for the same period.

Fines --
 A charge of 10 cents is made for each
day a book is kept overtime.

—— **WATCH THE DATE DUE** ——

JAMES BUCHANAN

ENCYCLOPEDIA
of PRESIDENTS

James Buchanan

Fifteenth President of the United States

By Marlene Targ Brill

Consultant: Charles Abele, Ph.D.
Social Studies Instructor
Chicago Public School System

CHILDRENS PRESS ®

CHICAGO

FOR PRESIDENT
JAMES BUCHANAN.

JAMES BUCHANAN.
FOR VICE-PRESIDENT
JOHN C. BRECKINRIDGE.

We Po'ked 'em in '44.
We Pierced 'em in '52.
And we'll " Buck 'em" in '56.

A Democratic campaign
badge for the 1856
presidential race

Library of Congress Cataloging-in-Publication Data

Brill, Marlene Targ.
  James Buchanan / by Marlene Targ Brill.
    p.   cm. — (Encyclopedia of presidents)
  Includes index.
  Summary: Describes the early life and political career of the
man who served as president in the years just before the Civil
War.
  ISBN 0-516-01358-0
  1.   Buchanan, James, 1791-1868—Juvenile
literature.   2.   Presidents—United States—Biography—
Juvenile literature.   3.   United States—Politics and
government—1857-1861—Juvenile literature.
[1. Buchanan, James, 1791-1868.   2.   Presidents.]
I. Title. II. Series.
E437.B78   1988
973.6'8'0924—dc19   88-10884
[B]   CIP
[92]   AC

Childrens Press®, Chicago
Copyright ©1988 by Regensteiner Publishing Enterprises, Inc.
All rights reserved. Published simultaneously in Canada.
Printed in the United States of America.
1 2 3 4 5 6 7 8 9 10 R 97 96 95 94 93 92 91 90 89 88

Picture Acknowledgments

Joseph E. Barrett, Courtesy U.S. Capitol
Historical Society—14

The Bettmann Archive—4, 8, 25, 34, 42
(bottom), 44, 46, 70, 72, 73, 89

Historical Pictures Service, Chicago—5, 15, 18,
20, 22 (3 pictures), 30, 32, 33, 38, 42 (top), 43
(2 pictures), 45, 54 (2 pictures), 55 (top), 58, 68,
71, 78 (2 pictures), 79 (2 pictures), 82, 83, 84,
88

Kansas State Historical Society, Topeka—9

Courtesy Library of Congress—6, 55 (bottom),
57, 62 (top), 63 (2 pictures), 65, 75 (bottom), 80,
81

Courtesy National Park Service—75 (top)

North Wind Picture Archives—12, 27, 37
(upper), 39

Courtesy U.S. Bureau of Printing and
Engraving—2, 37 (lower), 51, 52 (2 pictures)

Vision Quest—62 (bottom)

Cover design and illustration
by Steven Gaston Dobson

The two sides of a medal
commemorating the inauguration
of James Buchanan in 1857

Table of Contents

Chapter 1

Plot against the President

"And what is the nature of the investigation . . . ?" demanded President James Buchanan in an angry letter to Congress. "It is as vague and general as the English language affords words in which to make it."

The fifteenth president of the United States was enraged at the House of Representatives. How could they even think there was misconduct within his administration? How could they take the word of Congressman John Covode, who suggested Buchanan's wrongdoing?

Worse yet, how could they appoint a secret committee headed by Covode to pry into his presidency? This was the first committee ever established to review a U.S. president, and there was not even any proof of misdeed. Buchanan protested: "To make the accuser the judge is a violation of . . . justice, and is condemned by the practice of all civilized nations."

The House of Representatives rejected Buchanan's objections. His enemies clearly wanted him out of the way for the next election. They wanted his downfall now. Groups from each party saw him as the reason the Democratic party and the nation were splitting apart.

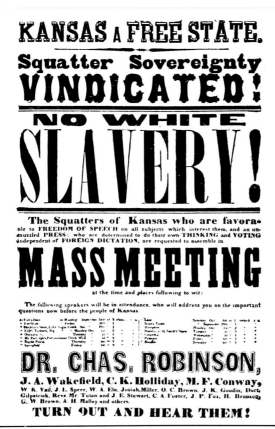

A poster announcing "mass meetings" on Kansas's hotly debated slavery issue

Northern Democrats and the new Republicans were after Buchanan for his seemingly strong stand in favor of slavery. Buchanan agreed with the Supreme Court's decision in the Dred Scott case, which had left Congress and the courts without power over slavery in the territories. Buchanan also supported Kansas's entering the Union as a slave state. His main concern was to balance slave and free states in the Union.

Southern Democrats believed Buchanan had not gone far enough to quiet antislavery fanatics. They felt his weak attempts to uphold slavery led to more violence in Kansas and to abolitionist John Brown's raid on a federal arsenal at Harpers Ferry, Virginia. Southerners also believed Brown was aided by abolitionist Republicans. The Covode Commission could be used to discredit proslavery Democrats and the president before election.

8

Abolitionist John Brown, who led the raid on Harpers Ferry

Buchanan was doomed no matter what he did. From the first day of his presidency, the slavery issue was a thorn in his side. Personally, Buchanan thought slavery "a great political and great moral evil." However, as a conservative lawyer, he followed the Constitution and its interpretations by the courts without question.

The president agreed that people should not own slaves. But the courts maintained in the Dred Scott case that slaves were property and did not have any rights under the Constitution. Slaves were the personal matter of their owners, not any business of troublemaking northern abolitionists.

Buchanan believed slavery was beyond the powers of government. Unfortunately for Buchanan, slave owners and abolitionists disagreed. Each side wanted to impose its will on the other.

States began banding together. New states joining the Union were forced to declare their position on slavery. The more power the free states gained, the more the slave states felt the Union did not serve their interests. The country was pulling apart.

Buchanan wanted Congress to pass new laws before he could act for or against slavery. He saw his job in office as peacemaker. He believed a balance between slavery and antislavery factions would satisfy both sides. Then the problem would gradually fade away.

The president was a patient man, a voice of calm among the excited and angry foes. He was sure his forty-three years in politics would help him unify the country. Before the 1856 election, his northern and southern supporters agreed. His campaign slogan was "Buchanan and the Union."

No other politician at the time had the experience that Buchanan had. He had served in state government, in both houses of Congress, as secretary of state, and as minister to Russia and England. He had taken part in expanding United States territories, creating treaties with foreign countries, beginning construction on the transcontinental railroad, and enlarging the army and navy. He had sent a message over the first transatlantic cable to Queen Victoria of England. But few presidents had entered office in such trying times.

The patience that earned Buchanan the presidency became his weakness. Congress had become frustrated with an impossible situation and a seemingly inactive president.

Investigators on the Covode Commission reached into every corner of the administration, hoping to build a case against Buchanan and the Democrats. They recorded almost eight hundred pages of questioning. In their thirty-page report, the committee told of payoffs and poor business deals that were typical in most administrations for the last twenty years.

But the committee found that the president had broken no laws. For Buchanan, the report cleared his name. Nevertheless, the suggestion of improper acts cast a shadow over the rest of his presidency.

The American people had lost their confidence and trust in Buchanan, both as a person and as an administrator. He no longer had the support of Congress nor of the public at large.

The Covode Committee did little to change the course of history. However, at the time, the investigation struck a heavy blow to Buchanan, to American politics, and to the people of the United States. Buchanan had seen himself as a great peacemaker. His task had been to keep both sides happy, keep the South in the Union, and keep the country moving forward.

Instead, critics from all sides saw him as a weak, out-dated old man who was bungling his presidency. They saw him as someone helpless to patch up the Union that was crumbling before him.

The growing town of Washington, D.C., in 1800

Chapter 2

Birth of a President

Even before becoming a nation, the United States struggled with the question of slavery. Initially, colonists brought slaves from the West Indies to work land in the North and South. In the South, slaves provided cheap human labor for large plantations. However, the colder, less fertile land and the growing cities reduced the need for slave labor in the North. Gradually, religious northerners began to view slave ownership as sinful.

Once the colonists won freedom from England, there were other, more pressing issues. Their leaders molded the economy, the court system, and foreign policy. Those opposed to slavery worked out compromises with slave owners.

By 1791, President George Washington led a thriving country. With the latest addition of Vermont, there were fourteen states in the Union and nearly four million people. The Bill of Rights—the first ten amendments to the Constitution, guaranteeing rights of free speech, press, religion, and assembly—had just gone into effect. Federalist and Republican party politicians exchanged attacks in city newspapers. And the Supreme Court met for the first time. With strong government and a national bank to encourage trade, the economy prospered.

The Philadelphia wharves in 1800, as the government moves from there to Washington, D. C.

Still, there were few large cities beyond New York, Philadelphia, Baltimore, and Boston. The nation's capital moved from New York City to temporary quarters in the more cosmopolitan city of Philadelphia. A permanent capital for the United States was under construction in swampland along the Potomac River between George Town, Maryland, and Alexandria, Virginia. Designed like the spokes of a wheel, it reflected the three branches of government, with main buildings for the president, the Supreme Court, and Congress. George Washington called the new capital "Federal City." But city planners renamed it "Washington" after their great leader.

A pioneer hunter in the new American wilderness

Most of the country was rural, and nine out of ten people farmed. The only manufactured goods were handmade in homes and storefronts. An industrious man could do well, no matter what his background.

Such was the case for James Buchanan's father. At age twenty-two, the elder James had sailed to the United States from Ireland to seek his fortune. He secured a job at a little trading post called Stony Batter about forty miles west of Philadelphia in Cove Gap.

The area was wilderness. Nevertheless, the post was an important meeting point on the road between Philadelphia and Pittsburgh, Pennsylvania. On some days, as many as one hundred horses rested in stables there. So many goods passed from the city to the western frontier that the trading post owner built a warehouse for storage.

After four years, Buchanan had the chance to buy Stony Batter. The clever young man now owned log cabins, barns, stables, a storehouse, fields for farming, and an orchard. With land and a business, he was ready in 1788 to marry his twenty-one-year-old sweetheart, Elizabeth Speers, and start a family.

Within a year the Buchanans' first child, Mary, was born. On April 23, 1791, the couple rejoiced again with the birth of their first son, whom they named after his father. Their happiness was short-lived, however, as baby Mary died within that year. Little James assumed a special place in the family that would always remain. He was the first of eleven children to survive babyhood and the only son for the next fourteen years.

As the family grew, Stony Batter prospered. Nonetheless, Elizabeth longed for a quieter life. Stony Batter, with its rowdy travelers and constant wagon and horse traffic, became a difficult place to raise children.

By 1794, the elder Buchanan earned enough money to buy a three-hundred-acre piece of land five miles to the east, near Mercersburg. He placed his brother-in-law in charge of the trading post and moved the family by wagon. Soon he bought a two-story brick building in the center of town. The building served as both a home and a store.

Mercersburg proved an ideal spot for the Buchanans. Rolling farmland dotted with oak trees surrounded the quaint village and made a lovely sight. In these peaceful and more orderly surroundings, young James learned a love for the land that stayed with him forever. And for the first time the boy had playmates other than his sisters.

Until then, James and his sisters received their education from their mother. Although unschooled, Elizabeth read widely from John Milton, Alexander Pope, and other writers of the day. She told wonderful stories, particularly of the family hero, George Washington. But her greatest influence on James came from her strict Presbyterian teachings. A strong belief in God's will and the Ten Commandments guided Elizabeth and her children through the most difficult times.

Elizabeth taught the girls to cook, can, spin, weave, sew, and knit. As was the custom then, girls learned only enough reading and writing to be able to handle social letters. But Elizabeth and her husband expected more of James. As eldest son, he was to seek a profession.

The elder James was a stern force in his boy's life. James worked with his father in the store. His father was proud of the boy's quick mind and his talent beyond his years. But he never praised the boy. He checked young James's every job to make sure it was done correctly. James both respected and feared his father, but he never found him a loving friend.

Working in the store greatly influenced Buchanan's character. Here he learned the value of money and of keeping accurate records. In time he developed into an exacting young man, neatly recording almost every penny he spent or saved and keeping a detailed diary.

Later, as ambassador to Great Britain, he accounted for the smallest exchanges, including his valet's purchases of pins and suspender buttons. Even as president, he wrote a check for three cents to cover an error in a grocer's bill.

Dickinson College in Carlisle, Pennsylvania

The store also provided James with his first view of politics. Because his father was a merchant, landowner, and town leader, men often gathered in the store to discuss events of the day. By his early teens, James joined these discussions. He also accepted his father's preference for the Federalist party. This was George Washington's political party, and it favored a strong Union.

Thanks to his father's success, James received a good education. At Old Stone Academy grammar school, James studied advanced English, Latin, and Greek, as well as reading, writing, and math. James was a good student—so good that he entered Dickinson College in Carlisle, Pennsylvania, as a junior at the age of sixteen.

James's mother had wanted her son to be a minister. However, his father wanted him to make money to support their growing family in case he should die. In the early 1800s, there was money to be made from land sales. Buyers and sellers needed lawyers to arrange and protect their deals. So James's father advised him to study law.

At first, James attended to his studies at Dickinson. But classmates mocked his hard work. To make friends, James joined and even led others in merrymaking. In his diary he admitted, "... in order to be considered a clever and spirited youth, I engaged in every sort of ... mischief."

Despite his drinking, cigar smoking, and keeping late hours—all against school rules—James still earned good grades. He easily excelled in Latin, Greek, mathematics, geography, literature, philosophy, and history.

By the end of his first year, the college threatened to expel James for disorderly conduct. The family minister from Mercersburg, who was also a Dickinson trustee, spoke in James's favor. James finished another year at Dickinson and graduated with honors. But further challenges to school authority caused James's professors to keep the highest honor of valedictorian from him.

His disappointed father scolded him for crossing his elders. He further warned that "the more you know of mankind, the more you will distrust them."

James left Dickinson "feeling little attachment for the Alma Mater." However, his brush with school authorities left him with a deep respect for the law. Later, as president, he would try to make peace between the states by declaring, "I acknowledge no master but the law."

Chapter 3

Making of a Politician

To the young graduate, the world was constantly changing. Europe was in the midst of the Napoleonic wars. At
home, inventions of the steam engine, cotton gin, ice
refrigerator, and mass production were slowly altering
everyday life and the economy.

To keep production high, some countries imported more
slaves and hired children for labor. The cotton gin, in par-
ticular, affected slave trade in the southern United States.
Because the machine cleaned cotton so quickly, plantations
needed more slaves to handle larger cotton harvests.

By 1809, many countries had introduced laws to protect
individual rights. Great Britain forbade hiring children
under nine years of age and prohibited their working in
factories for more than twelve hours a day. France out-
lawed slavery. And the United States enacted a law against
importing slaves, which many states ignored.

As a student, Buchanan had only dabbled in world
issues. Now his thoughts were on healing his hurt pride
and deciding where to study law. James spent two months
after graduation at home hunting squirrels for his favorite
stew and thinking about his future.

Opposite page: James Buchanan as a young man

Above: Child laborers making twine

Left: Eli Whitney's cotton gin

Below: The Stourbridge Lion, an eight-ton steam locomotive

James's father soon decided the next step for his son. In December 1809, James boarded a stagecoach bound for Lancaster, Pennsylvania. He was to learn law as a clerk for James Hopkins, leader of the Lancaster bar.

As the capital of Pennsylvania and the biggest inland city in the United States, Lancaster boasted a population of six thousand, rich farms, and a booming iron industry. Shops and taverns with carved signs of animals, national heroes, and Indian heads lined city streets.

Lancaster newspapers warned of runaway slaves and wives, announced sales of local farms, and printed sermons. There were ads for Dr. Robertson's Vegetable Nervous Cordial, separate dancing classes for men and women, and rooms at the Brighton Hotel with "convenient Baths."

James located a room at Widow Duchman's Inn near the courthouse and main city square. Here some of the most powerful families in Pennsylvania lived. Although a poor clerk, James believed his closeness to judges, the governor, and wealthy iron king Robert Coleman would bring him good fortune, too.

At first, the lively life in Lancaster taverns attracted James. But his father warned him "not to be carried off by the many amusements . . . in that place." In fact, the elder James wrote letters cautioning his son's every move.

For the next three years James studied law day and night. His only rest was to stroll in the woods at the end of the day. Here he created speeches about what he had learned that day. On these walks, James practiced public speaking skills that would later win him praise as a lawyer and politician.

The year Congress declared war against Great Britain, opening the War of 1812, Hopkins agreed to sponsor James at the bar. In November 1812, James became a lawyer. Three months later he opened a law office near Widow Duchman's Inn and also got a job as deputy prosecutor for Lebanon County.

After two years' practice, James had earned only $1,096. To gain more clients, he decided to enter politics. The same day the British army marched on Washington, D.C., and threatened Baltimore, a Federalist friend nominated James for state representative of Lancaster County.

Like other Federalists, James disapproved of President Madison's handling of the War of 1812. However, he realized that politically he must defend his country. The day after his nomination, James gave a rousing patriotic speech. Then he volunteered for the militia to save Baltimore from the British.

The Lancaster County Dragoons, as James and his friends were called, never saw battle. Their only assignment was to acquire horses for the army, either by stealing or from volunteers. By the time his group completed its job, the British withdrew from Baltimore. Within a few weeks, the Dragoons were sent home and never called again. James became one of America's few leaders to remain a mere private.

Back in Lancaster, Buchanan easily won election as a state representative on the Federalist ticket. The thrill of being the Lancaster Federalists' first choice was dampened only by a letter from his father doubting the wisdom of temporarily leaving his law practice.

Harrisburg, the capital of Pennsylvania

Harrisburg, now the new state capital, proved a good training ground for the unskilled politician. James listened intently to speeches from the floor. After hearing many wandering talks, he decided to speak only after careful preparation.

Buchanan's first chance to air his ideas came during a debate over the state's military draft. Pennsylvania needed a strong army to defend the port of Philadelphia from British attack. Opposing groups argued over whether to establish volunteer troops or to draft some men to fight and make others pay for their upkeep.

Buchanan gave a spirited speech favoring volunteer forces. He argued that poor farmers in western Pennsylvania deserved the same privileges and duties as the rich minority in Philadelphia. James made an excellent plea, but it lost him favor among Federalists. A Democratic senator even suggested he switch parties.

Fortunately, news of peace with Britain ended the debate in February 1815. Nevertheless, reactions from the speech prompted James to keep his thoughts to himself for the rest of the term. James still worried about his chances for reelection.

This time, the senior Buchanan urged his son to run in the 1815 election. Contacts made through the legislature would earn James more than $2,000 that year. James was making a name for himself in local politics. With more seasoning, the elder Buchanan believed, James could move on to the United States Congress.

To prove his Federalist loyalties, James addressed the Independence Day rally of Lancaster's Washington Association. His tall, strong build, delicate features, blond hair, and sharp blue eyes made a striking impression on the audience. He drew their attention, too, by his habit of cocking his head to adjust the vision between his one far-sighted eye and one nearsighted eye. More important, James's fiery story of America's break from Great Britain, with harsh criticism of President Madison and the Democratic Congress, excited listeners in the village square.

Buchanan easily won reelection to the Pennsylvania house of representatives. But the strong charges he made during his speech angered local Democrats and those Federalists who were sympathetic to their causes. From now on, Buchanan learned to moderate his statements.

In the fall of 1815, the main issue for the legislature was the rechartering of the national bank. The original national bank charter had run out before the War of 1812.

President James Madison

Effects of foreign trade blockades and the cost of war reduced the country's ability to back up its paper money. States passed various laws concerning the handling of money. By 1815, so many people had lost faith in United States paper currency that they only did business with gold coins or exchange of goods.

James sided with President Madison, agreeing that a central bank put too much control in the hands of a few. Opponents, including many Federalists, argued that a national bank restored a strong system of currency.

By the end of his term, Buchanan was not sure he agreed with his party's beliefs. Also, according to local custom, representatives had to step down after two terms. Buchanan was relieved to be able to turn to his law practice once again.

Over the next four years, James devoted himself to arguing criminal and civil cases, settling estates, and handling property. His arguments were so detailed and so well planned that judges overlooked their length.

Some thought of him as a "hair splitter" because he was so thorough. One Lancaster judge later wrote of the young attorney: "He was cut out by nature for a great lawyer, and I think was spoiled by fortune when she made him a statesman."

At twenty-five, young Buchanan had a chance to defend a Federalist judge against impeachment charges. The Democratic Pennsylvania legislature wanted all Federalist judges removed from the bench. They charged that this judge had ruled improperly in a lawsuit. James's skillful handling of this unpopular political case won him more clients.

By 1818, his income had risen to $8,000. James spent less time amusing himself in taverns and more time attending community affairs and eating dinners with Lancaster's elite. This handsome and successful six-footer was beginning to attract the attention of the young ladies of Lancaster.

In the winter of 1819, James and the rich and lovely Ann Coleman had a whirlwind courtship of parties and sleigh rides. By summer Ann agreed to marry James, against protests from her parents. Despite James's thriving legal practice, Ann's millionaire father, Robert Coleman, feared James was after the family fortune.

Gossip followed the prominent couple. As James became busier with law, rumors of his interest in money reached the Coleman household. At first, Ann dismissed the rumors as idle chatter. Then she heard that James had casually visited another young woman at a time he claimed to be too busy to see Ann.

Without hearing James's side, Ann broke the engagement. In despair, she left to visit her sister in Philadelphia—never to return alive. Some said she took an overdose of medicine, but there was never hard proof that she meant to take her own life.

News of Ann's death crushed the already saddened man. James wrote to her family asking to see the body and to mourn with them. His letters returned unopened. The Colemans and the town gossipers blamed James for Ann's death.

In one letter James said, ". . . the time will come when you will discover that she, as well as I, have been much abused. . . . I may sustain the shock of her death, but I feel that happiness has fled from me forever."

James had little energy for work and even less for facing the townspeople. After Ann's funeral he boarded a stagecoach for Mercersburg. Once he was home, family support and religious faith restored some of his energy and self-respect. He could return to Lancaster now. However, he would never be so near to marriage or feel the same about his future again.

Work did little to replace the loss James felt. He needed new direction. Change came in the form of a Federalist nomination to the United States House of Representatives. In November 1821, James joined Congress on Capitol Hill, where he devoted his energies for the next ten years.

James Buchanan

Chapter 4

From Representative
to Diplomat

Peace after the War of 1812 heralded a new age of progress. With strong feelings of nationalism, Americans were laying the foundation for greater liberty and prosperity. The country was experiencing worldwide recognition, expanded boundaries, cheaper transportation, and a growing economy. The Federalist party had declined, so the political scene was quiet. The early 1820s under President James Monroe became known as the "Era of Good Feeling."

The United States had twenty-three states and a population of 9.6 million people when President Monroe began his second term in 1821. New York had just passed Philadelphia as the nation's largest city. Large waves of immigrants swelled cities and forged frontiers, changing the face of these settlements.

Stopping for water on the westward trail

Many fur traders were entering the rugged new frontier areas in the North and the Northwest. They traded with Indians and sold their goods to company agents from the East. Like the Indians, these "mountain men" had to survive harsh conditions. Many thrived on their colorful life in the wild and remained to marry Indian women. Most settlements, however, grew between the Appalachian Mountains and Mississippi River. Eighty-three percent of Americans still relied on farming for their livelihood, and this area provided plenty of rich soil.

Settlers moving west in the nineteenth century

Settlers sought new territory with their families to escape overpopulation, poor soil, and increasing land prices. Women bravely tried to recapture the "civilized" life they had had in the East. But there were many adjustments to make and much hard work. Men and boys cut trees for cabins and firewood and cleared land for planting and harvesting crops. Women and girls made soap, clothes, and other goods. They also cared for the younger children, churned butter, prepared meals, preserved food for winter, and helped in the fields when needed. Often, the only tools brought from the East were axes, spades, and spinning wheels.

A group of ladies at a quilting bee

To complete all these tasks, frontier families without slaves learned to share their work. Several families would gather to sew quilts, husk corn, harvest wheat, raise a house, and roll logs. Drinking jugs of home brew added to the fun. Some of these festive social occasions became known as "bees."

New canals and roads opened land for speculation and trade. Some settlers clearly wanted to take advantage of cheaper, easier transportation to buy more land. The only obstacles were the Indians. Settlers wanted the Indians removed from what they viewed as their land. So the government developed a harder line against Indians. By the 1830s, federal and state governments pushed eastern Indian tribes west of the Mississippi River with bribes, tricks, and finally military force.

Treatment of Indians and slaves was contrary to the ideas fostered in the Constitution. But many white people really believed that they were superior. They believed they should be the sole heirs to the freedoms guaranteed in this great document.

Nowhere was debate over individual rights keener than in Washington, D.C. Southern states continued to rely on slave labor, and Washington was a port for slave ships. Potomac Park was originally a site of slave auctions.

Just before Buchanan came to the capital, argument sharpened over whether Missouri should be admitted to the Union as a slave state. Congress adopted the Missouri Compromise of 1820 as a temporary solution. The compromise banned slavery in Louisiana Purchase territory north of the 36°30' latitude, except for Missouri. Any states organized to the north would be admitted as free states. States south of this line could decide on slavery by popular vote, though it was assumed they would choose slavery. As a final compromise, Missouri entered the Union as a slave state to offset Maine's entry as a free state. Outwardly, these agreements seemed to appease both sides. However, the apparent calm of the 1820s was only a lull before the storm.

As Buchanan rode into Washington in November 1821, he felt the weight of responsibilities to his family, his law practice, and his new job. His father had died in the summer after being thrown from a carriage. James was in charge of the family estate and brothers and sisters were still at home. From now until his death he willingly cared for various members of his family.

James determined to be faithful to his voters. He also wanted to make a name for himself in Washington. For the next eight years Buchanan supported Pennsylvania's wishes for import duties on such goods as hemp, molasses, and iron, which were produced in the state. He softened Irish immigration laws, gained funds for local improvement projects, and promoted a system of public education.

Buchanan based his policies on the rights of individual farmers and manufacturers. He consistently championed equal rights for both the rich and the poor. Moreover, in accord with his views against a national banking system, many of his debates supported states' rights. After his first years in Congress, some wondered whether his leanings were Federalist, Democratic, or both. Fortunately, many of his voters wavered as well. The Federalist party had just about died out.

While in Congress, Buchanan earned a reputation as someone with behind-the-scenes influence. He became known as a "fixer." In the disputed 1924 presidential election, friends called on him to figure out a way for the celebrated Tennessee senator, Andrew Jackson, to take office. Jackson won the most popular votes in the race against Secretary of State John Quincy Adams, but no candidate won a majority of electoral votes. Now the House of Representatives was to decide who would take office. Congressman Henry Clay, who had a strong following, could dictate many of the votes.

Pennsylvania congressmen were unsure how to vote. They urged Buchanan to talk to Jackson, a man he respected. Pennsylvanians opposed Adams because of his

Above: Statesman and
orator Henry Clay

Right: Secretary of State
John Quincy Adams

stand against tariffs. They wanted to know whether
Jackson planned to appoint Clay as secretary of state if
Clay supported Jackson for president.

In a brief meeting Jackson claimed he had made no
commitments. Buchanan pressed no further; he merely
related the news to his colleagues. But politics won the
election. The House of Representatives selected Adams as
president.

President Andrew Jackson

For the next two years, Buchanan fought against Adams for Jackson's issues. However, someone told Jackson a different story—that Buchanan was trying to make a deal for himself when he spoke to Jackson about the election. Jackson lashed out at Buchanan in the *Lancaster Journal* about his "bargain and sale." The two exchanged angry articles for months.

As the tempest died down, Buchanan was hurt that Jackson could believe such lies. He still supported Jackson's ideas about popular government. But he became extremely cautious about political schemes.

In the 1828 election, Buchanan reorganized his Pennsylvania followers to support Jackson. This time Jackson became president, with John C. Calhoun as his vice-president. The country celebrated Jackson as the "people's

A "hickory pole" campaign parade for Andrew Jackson

choice." Seventy-eight percent of adult males who could vote did, as opposed to 27 percent in 1824. Buchanan solidly supported Jackson's election, so he easily won his seat in Congress on Jackson's coattails.

The campaign of 1828 was an unusually dirty one, bringing up "bargain and sale" and other slanderous remarks. Some newspapers quoted Buchanan as saying a judge's wife was born out of wedlock. Others told cruel rumors about Jackson's wife.

Stress from the election left Buchanan with an attack of bilious fever, a recurring liver disease he had had since his teens. He longed for a rest—one that would take him back to his neglected law practice. But this was not to happen before he made one of his greatest contributions to the United States.

As chairman of the House Judiciary Committee, Buchanan spoke out against a proposal to abolish part of the Judiciary Act of 1789. The act affirmed the authority of the national court system. After a brilliant plea, the House voted 138 to 51 in favor of Buchanan's unpopular stand and preserved the power of the Supreme Court.

As Buchanan went home to Lancaster after this session of Congress, there was some speculation about his running for vice-president in the next election. He did not encourage these suggestions, and nothing came of them. However, President Jackson recognized the benefit of Buchanan's support.

Partly to reward Buchanan and partly to limit his leadership role within the Pennsylvania Democratic party, Jackson offered Buchanan the position of minister to the Russian court at Saint Petersburg. At first, Buchanan rejected the offer. But further prodding helped Buchanan to view the job as his political duty.

The next year was busy for Buchanan. He took care of his law practice, real estate, and investments. He paid rent for his pew at the English Presbyterian Church. And he visited his mother in Mercersburg, a visit that proved to be their last meeting. Then he left for Washington to receive instructions and his $9,000-a-year pay.

His heart was heavy now. He would miss Lancaster. He feared he was leaving "the most free and happy country on earth for a despotism more severe than any which exists in Europe." Indeed, he would find the basic freedoms of speech, press, and unopened mail lacking under the Russian emperor Nicholas I.

Little did Buchanan know that on August 22 of that same year, a black preacher named Nat Turner would lead a group of slaves on a rampage that killed sixty Virginia slave owners. Reactions to the uprising were swift. Scared owners hanged the rebels. New laws greatly limited slaves' rights to travel, assemble for meetings, and even read and write. But white people in the United States saw no comparison between these ills and those of other countries like Russia.

The twenty-five-day sailing voyage from New York to Liverpool, England, left James weak from seasickness but happy to arrive safely. He spent two weeks touring England with the enthusiasm of a child. James traveled between Liverpool and Manchester by train, describing the trip as "a distance of 30 miles—in one hour and twenty-five minutes."

Saint Petersburg astounded Buchanan. In 1832 the Russian capital was one of the liveliest cultural centers of the world. Its grand buildings, built more than a century earlier by Peter the Great, towered over the main streets and Neva River.

Life for a Russian diplomat was quite formal and expensive. Buchanan lived in a large villa with a "courtyard, stables for six horses, a carriage, and sleigh house, and special apartment for servants." He was expected to dress formally and to ride a four-horse carriage to the Russian court. The carriage driver dressed in Russian costume and wore a long, black beard. Attending soldiers had considerably more plumage. James would have to stretch his salary to pay for all these extras.

Above: Nat Turner and his associates plan their rebellion

Left: A woodcut showing Nat Turner's capture

Two artists' views of the Russian capital of Saint Petersburg
during the time James Buchanan served there as U.S. minister

Russian emperor Nicholas I calming a riot during a cholera outbreak in 1831

The Russian ministry gave Buchanan the opportunity to be an international "fixer." His two jobs were to negotiate a commerce treaty opening trade between Russia and the United States and to bargain for a maritime treaty that would insure safe passage of United States ships and crews.

For almost two years Buchanan played a political game between rival ministers, Count Nesselrode and Baron Krudener. The maritime treaty was never reached. However, Buchanan negotiated the first commercial agreement of its kind with the imperial government. American and Russian ships received "most-favored-nation" status in each other's ports. Russia earned a friend to balance England's

Nicholas I, Russian czar (emperor) from 1825 to 1855

strength at sea. And the United States gained new sources of trade and a coveted place in western politics.

After signing the treaty, Buchanan requested permission to go home. His mother and his favorite brother had died, and another brother and sister had taken marriage partners without his knowledge. Also, friends had written that he would be a good candidate for the Senate. If he left Russia soon, he could be home in time to run in the next senatorial election.

As Buchanan left Russia, Emperor Nicholas I told him to tell President Jackson to "send him another minister exactly like the one leaving that day."

America in the 1830s: Country ways and city ways converge.

Chapter 5

The Age of the People

The evening that James's ship, the *Susquehanna*, docked in Philadelphia harbor, his friends honored him with a five-dollar-a-plate dinner celebration. Could his popularity sweep him all the way to the Senate, maybe even the presidency?

Within two weeks Buchanan realized he had lost some influence while overseas. In his first race for United States senator he was defeated—the only election defeat in his career. Some say he bowed to pressure from Jackson to keep harmony in state politics. Whatever the reason, Buchanan took the next year to rebuild his following, reestablish his law practice, and attend to personal matters.

James moved into the old Coleman house, where he had once visited Ann. This gave him a strange feeling indeed. Although he became interested in another Lancaster woman around this time, the romance, as with several others, amounted to little. But what he needed most at this time was a housekeeper to manage his home while he was away in Washington, D.C. Miss Hetty, the twenty-eight-year-old niece of a Lancaster innkeeper, was just the person he needed.

Soon Buchanan had his chance for Senate victory. President Jackson appointed Senator Wilkins of Pennsylvania as Russian ambassador. On December 15, 1834, Buchanan qualified for Wilkins's empty Senate seat and set off for Washington.

In the two years that James had spent overseas, politics and the country entered a new age—the age of democracy and the common man. More people had access to more freedoms than ever before in the Western world. Any white man could raise himself from poverty to wealth and influence. Family connections brought fewer of the automatic privileges of earlier days. European nobles visiting America were constantly offended by customs and attitudes of "democratic" men and women. There was no first-class steamboat or railroad travel. Rich and poor alike ate and slept under the same roofs at country inns and even some city hotels.

Laws stripped away most barriers to voting. Previously, and in most European countries, property ownership dictated who could vote. Here all white men could vote, with or without land. Women, blacks, and Indians, however, were still left without voting rights.

With expanded numbers of voters came new ways to lure votes. In every county of every state, politicians made speeches, held rallies, parades, and picnics, and handed out tokens of their campaigns. For the first time, national conventions with state delegates became the way to select presidential candidates.

Eastern cities spawned the first workingmen's parties and trade unions. Workers wanted equal rights in the form of higher wages and greater control over what they produced. Wealthy industrialists were seen as a threat to democracy.

Worker dissatisfaction led to a movement for expanding public education. Education was seen as a way to narrow the gap between rich and poor. It was also an outgrowth of a more "child-centered" approach to raising children. People began to see children as individuals instead of miniature adults, with needs different than their parents'. To give more care to each child individually, parents had reduced average family sizes from seven children in the early 1800s to five.

Even styles of dress blurred the lines between classes. Men of all classes replaced their wigs and knee breeches with short hair and long pants. Similarly, servant girls wore long dresses in the style of gowns worn by wealthier women.

Politicians at this time felt compelled to reward their loyal party members. Senator William Marcy of New York noted that "to the victors belong the spoils of the enemy." This statement gave the name "spoils system" to the practice of rewarding supporters with government jobs. Many high government officials at this time made a habit of offering jobs "to enrich their friends," a habit approved by Jackson.

The two main issues during Buchanan's time in the Senate were banking and slavery. The growing problems over rechartering the national bank and finding a place for federal funds gravely altered the economy over the next ten years.

Jackson's fight against the "monster corporation" of the national bank became quite heated. Angry procharter men such as senators Henry Clay, John C. Calhoun, and Daniel Webster split to form their own party, eventually known as the Whigs. They ridiculed Jackson as "King Andrew" for his domineering way of handling banking and all national problems.

Buchanan was in an awkward position regarding national banking. His electors wanted federal funds to remain in Pennsylvania, where the national bank had been. Pennsylvania Democrats worried that money would go to New York because of Jackson's political connections with Martin Van Buren. Van Buren was the former New York governor and Jackson's hand-picked candidate for next president. New York was already pulling ahead of Philadelphia as the nation's leading trade center.

But being a good Democrat meant being a Jacksonian. Buchanan decided that his political future was more secure if he supported "Old Hickory" than if he fought to preserve the bank.

Buchanan tried to satisfy both sides. He spoke several times on Jackson's behalf. On the state level, Buchanan encouraged competing groups to be loyal to Van Buren in the 1836 election. When issues became too heated, he stepped back.

As recognized leader of the Democrats, Buchanan reunited enough Pennsylvanians to back Van Buren and elect him to his own six-year Senate seat. This was the first time since he entered politics that Buchanan knew he had a long-term job.

President Martin Van Buren

The financial trouble left by Jackson only got worse under Van Buren. Before leaving office, Jackson had signed legislation ordering all federal money removed from the national bank and put in state banks. Many state banks printed their own paper money. Then they lent it to land speculators who bought up western land, hoping to sell it to settlers at a profit. This flood of paper money resulted in inflation, or higher prices because of a drop in the value of money. Jackson quickly curbed the inflation by requiring only gold or silver to be used to purchase land. The resulting Panic of 1837 was followed by a great slump in trade, credit, land sales, and jobs.

Above: William Henry Harrison,
who died after a month in office

Right: John Tyler, who became
president after Harrison's death

Buchanan proposed a special federal agency to collect
and pay money. Van Buren liked the idea and used it for
his own "subtreasury" bill, which Buchanan applauded.
The bill passed in the Senate but not the House until 1840.
By 1841, the economic turmoil put Van Buren out of
office, and General William Henry Harrison became the
first Whig president. But within a month the old general
died, leaving Vice-President John Tyler in command.

Meanwhile, the abolition movement was gaining
ground. During the calm of the 1820s, many Americans
admitted slavery was wrong. But they saw no chance for
change unless slave owners freed their slaves on their own.
Organizations like the American Colonization Society
called for moving freed blacks to a colony of their own in
Liberia, West Africa. This would relieve slave owners who
feared that freed slaves would cause a race war.

By 1831, free northern blacks and white abolitionists rejected the idea of the Liberian colony. They hoped to make racial equality a reality in the United States. Groups like the American Anti-Slavery Society sprang up to battle slavery. Boston minister William Lloyd Garrison published a weekly antislavery journal called the *Liberator*.

In turn, southerners and some northerners developed stronger feelings against abolitionists. Garrison and other abolitionist groups often met with violence. A Quaker abolitionist, Prudence Crandall, was imprisoned for admitting black girls to her girls' school.

Buchanan took many stands against slavery, which he detested. In contrast, he also upheld slave owners' rights to their slaves' property and the states' rights to protect that property. Though he appeared to be flip-flopping, he was consistently voting in line with the Constitution.

At one point, the Senate moved to have the post office destroy any abolitionist writings that could incite slave riots. Daniel Webster argued that such a measure violated freedom of the press and mail. Buchanan defended freedom of the press, also. However, he contended that this was "a question not of property, but of public safety." Rebellious blacks could only do harm. The bill was defeated in spite of Buchanan's support.

Buchanan believed that abolitionists were "fanatics" who hurt the slave cause more than they helped it. Still, he defended their right to petition. As chairman of a Senate committee to study abolitionist petitions, Buchanan tried to keep the constitutional right to petition separate from the cause of slavery in the South.

OUR COUNTRY IS THE WORLD—OUR COUNTRYMEN ARE ALL MANKIND.

BOSTON, MASS., FRIDAY, JUNE 14, 1850.

The pictorial heading of
the abolitionist newspaper
The Liberator (above),
published by William Lloyd
Garrison (left)

**Above: Quaker
abolitionist and
schoolteacher
Prudence Crandall,
who was imprisoned
for admitting
black girls to
her school**

Right: Daniel Webster

Most of the five hundred petitions from antislavery societies concerned banning slavery and slave trade in the capital and the territories. Southerners considered Washington, D.C., one of their strongholds. Banning slavery here was the same as attacking the entire South.

Now Buchanan found himself fighting Calhoun and other proslavery senators. Buchanan came down hard on the side of the Constitution. He argued, "We have just as little right to interfere with slavery in the South, as we have to touch the right of petition."

To compromise, Buchanan suggested accepting the petitions but rejecting their content. Two months of debate later, the Senate passed his motion. The battle to keep both sides satisfied was won for a while. But the smoldering war was not over yet. Senator King of Alabama, Buchanan's Washington roommate, warned that northerners must curb their protests or "we will separate from them."

Buchanan's career in the Senate was solid but never brilliant. His views on foreign and domestic policy were constant. He followed the established laws to the letter. Anyone who thought otherwise was a "ruffian" and "spoiler." He never had his own agenda, only that of others in his party. His job was to support, balance, and fix — a role that gained him the respect of his associates but little notice among voters outside his state.

Even within his family, this role persisted. There were so many brothers, sisters, and offspring that James often compared his family to politics. As eldest brother, James handled family finances, calmed feuds among members, and was guardian for half a dozen nieces and nephews.

President James Knox Polk

By 1839, six-year-old nephew James Buchanan Henry and nine-year-old niece Harriet Lane moved into the old Coleman home with Miss Hetty after their parents died. James told Miss Hetty to buy more furniture to suit the growing brood and a $17.50 piano for Harriet to play. James proved a stern but loving guardian.

By now, James clearly wanted the presidential nomination in 1844. But he wanted to be asked. When James K. Polk seemed to be the favorite, Buchanan withdrew his name rather than fight. Instead, he contented himself with a third Senate term and worked for Polk's election.

When election returns were counted, Polk was pleased to carry Pennsylvania. He knew whom to thank for the votes. Within a month, Buchanan received a letter inviting him to be secretary of state in Polk's cabinet.

Chapter 6

Bound for the Presidency

Buchanan became secretary of state in 1845. Unfortunately, this meant spending more time in Washington than in the more refined Lancaster countryside he loved.

Construction of the nation's capital was progressing slower than city planners had intended. Streets were still cluttered with chickens, geese, and pigs, and roads were full of potholes. City canals smelled foul. Slave pens stood a mile from the Capitol building. Not far away, an abolitionist network called the Underground Railroad helped slaves escape to free lands.

To be a cabinet member, James needed a home fit for formal state functions. He rented an elegant house near the State Department building for $2,000 a year. Then he began wading through the disorganized department he inherited. James had to give out jobs of postmasters, prison wardens, lighthouse keepers, and more before attending to President Polk's official agenda.

Polk's election brought new hope of party and national unity. His platform championed greater expansion of the United States. He believed that the national fervor to acquire Oregon from Great Britain and California from Mexico would draw attention from the slavery issue.

Just before the election, Congress gave approval for Texas to join the Union. This fit Polk's policy of expanding the country from shore to shore. But it upset abolitionists who feared that expansion was a patriotic hoax to get more slave states into the Union. In addition, Mexico refused to recognize Texas's independence. The United States and Mexico disagreed over the location of Texas's southern border, and Mexico was ready to go to war in protest.

To pacify abolitionists, Polk hoped to gain the territory of Oregon from the British as a free region. The Oregon Territory had been settled jointly by the United States and Great Britain since 1827. The United States claimed land north to the 54°40′ latitude. Britain countered that the area was theirs, including British Columbia, present-day Washington State, and parts of Montana and Idaho.

In the 1820s, there was little trouble over these boundaries. Few trappers came to the area. As settlers came to farm, the question of land rights became more critical. In July 1845, Polk empowered Buchanan to propose the forty-ninth parallel as the northern boundary of the United States, leaving British Columbia to the British. When the British rejected the offer, Polk pressed for the entire territory all the way to the 54°40′ line.

Buchanan and Polk often disagreed about how and when to proceed with negotiations. Immediately Polk wanted to cut off talks with Britain. Buchanan was calmer in his approach. He did not want the United States to appear weak. However, he needed peace with Britain at a time when war with Mexico looked certain.

In the end Buchanan, working behind the scenes, secured the original compromise offer for the United States. A year after negotiations began, the United States signed a treaty securing the Oregon Territory up to the forty-ninth parallel. For the first time, the United States firmly held land on the Pacific coast.

As Buchanan dickered with Britain, hostilities increased with Mexico. In March 1845, diplomatic relations between the two countries ended. Texans looked to Washington for help as Mexican troops amassed along the border.

Polk ordered Buchanan back from vacation to prepare for war with Mexico. From this Polk hoped to gain New Mexico and California, in addition to Texas. Buchanan cautioned Polk to let Mexico fire the first shots. The rest of the world was watching. The United States must not appear aggressive. On May 11, 1946, Mexico gave Polk his chance to declare war.

For the next two years, generals Zachary Taylor and Winfield Scott fought their way into Mexico. Mexicans had no choice but to bargain. Polk wanted all of Mexico for his troubles. But Buchanan persuaded him to be content with a treaty that gave the United States Texas, California, and other territory in the Southwest in exchange for fifteen million dollars.

Although Buchanan lacked real power as secretary of state, he was able to display his diplomatic talents. He settled the Oregon dispute peacefully and fought to avoid war with Mexico. He worked tirelessly to maintain solid relations with other major powers, but his long hours brought little reward.

Above: Winfield Scott's troops
bombard Vera Cruz, Mexico

Left: General Winfield Scott

**Above: Invasion
of Mexico City**

**Right: General
Zachary Taylor**

Buchanan wanted the Supreme Court judgeship that Polk had offered to him earlier. He had turned it down because the president needed him during the war with Mexico. If he could not join the Supreme Court, he hoped to receive the next presidential nomination instead. However, the Democratic choice in 1848 was Lewis Cass of Michigan, who lost to the Whig candidate, General Zachary Taylor. By the end of his term as secretary, Buchanan was sick, tired, and glad to leave the State Department.

After almost thirty years of public service, Buchanan looked forward to retirement. He welcomed the company of his twenty-two nieces and nephews and thirteen grandnieces and grandnephews. Seven of the children were orphans under his direct care, and several others looked to him as a parent. He would buy a larger home where he could enjoy them and look toward the 1852 election.

In the summer of 1848 Buchanan purchased a lovely twenty-two-acre country estate called Wheatland, a mile and a half west of Lancaster, Pennsylvania. Rich, rolling meadows surrounded the plain red-brick villa. At Wheatland, Buchanan lived the genteel life of a southern gentleman and enjoyed simple, quiet amusements. He read from his large library, tended the garden, decorated the house, and delighted in his family and friends.

Here Buchanan became known as the "Squire of Lancaster." At fifty-eight years of age, his white hair and tall, straight frame gave him a dignified look. His stiff, high collars and formal attire added to his polished appearance and friendly, polite nature. He fit in with any company — royalty or local tavern folk.

Wheatland, Buchanan's estate near Lancaster, Pennsylvania

Anyone visiting Wheatland was welcomed warmly with food, spirits, and hospitality. Buchanan particularly enjoyed giving sauerkraut and mashed potato dinners. Afterwards, he sipped Madeira wine and told stories of his travels to his adoring family. Harriet, now nineteen, presided over the many social activities for children at Wheatland. In summer, children "hunted eggs in the barn, went on straw rides, knocked peaches and pears from trees with sticks, or invaded the kitchen for fresh-made apple pie and milk."

Buchanan began inviting political friends to visit and discuss government events. Many loyal Democrats sought his advice. Wheatland, rather than the city, became Buchanan's "grand theatre of President making."

By the 1852 election, Buchanan had presidential fever. The only roadblock seemed to be his stand about the Compromise of 1850. The Compromise came after California applied for admission as a free state. Southerners feared that all the territories acquired from Mexico would prohibit slavery. The resulting concessions admitted California as a free state and prohibited buying and selling slaves in Washington, D.C. In return, southerners gained a tougher fugitive slave law for the return of runaway slaves. And the New Mexico and Utah territories were organized and allowed to decide upon slavery by vote.

Buchanan thought that the boundaries set by the Missouri Compromise should extend to California. He insisted that the Constitution already granted Congress all the powers it needed to control the territories. This power should not be abandoned and given to voters. However, he abided by the decision of Congress.

As the election approached, Buchanan's strict conservative views lost him support. Both parties chose generals who had been heroes of the Mexican War. General Winfield Scott became the Whig candidate, and General Franklin Pierce led the Democratic party to victory.

Pierce considered Buchanan a wise elder statesman. As such, he offered him the post of minister to England. He encouraged Buchanan to accept by telling him he was the only man to settle the problems at hand. The British ministry proved a difficult assignment. Britain was involved in the Crimean War with Russia, but the United States was too involved with issues at home to pay much attention to foreign problems.

The greatest successes in London went to Harriet, who had joined her uncle in the spring of 1854. The lively and talented young woman quickly won British hearts.

The queen found Harriet so delightful that she accorded her every courtesy of an ambassador's wife. Harriet was wined and dined. She even danced with Prince Albert. When Buchanan won an honorary degree with Alfred Lord Tennyson at Oxford University, it was Harriet who received students' cheers. As James said good-bye to the queen, her final words were about "dear Miss Lane."

Despite the lack of any clear progress, the British ministry worked to Buchanan's political advantage. He was out of the country when Congress passed the Kansas-Nebraska Act in 1854. The bill created two new territories from western land. It went contrary to the Missouri Compromise by allowing settlers there to decide whether to allow or ban slavery.

Northern and southern settlers flocked to these areas to gain control. The resulting violence resounded throughout the United States. Five abolitionists were killed in Lawrence, Kansas. Then antislavery extremist John Brown led a group that murdered five proslavery settlers. In Congress, Representative Preston Brooks of South Carolina beat Senator Charles Sumner of Massachusetts unconscious with a cane for his verbal attack on his proslavery uncle, Senator Butler.

Buchanan was one of the few politicians who did not get involved in the fight, at least not yet. His appeal to both sides as wise statesman would surely gain him the bid for president and win him the presidency.

Chapter 7

Mr. President

The 1856 race was the first presidential election to reflect deep sectional differences over slavery. Buchanan barely won the popular vote. However, a greater margin of electoral votes secured him the presidency.

Buchanan's strong showing in the South edged out ex-president Millard Fillmore. Fillmore, originally a Whig, ran as a member of the doomed Know-Nothing, or American, party. This party's main goal was to limit the flood of immigrants entering the United States. Fillmore's loss put an end to the Know-Nothings.

The biggest election surprise was the strong support for Republican John C. Frémont. Clearly, Republicans would be able to present a tough fight in the next election.

The day Buchanan took office, newspapers were debating equal education for women in coeducational schools, and Congress passed several bills. They lowered the import duties on iron, sugar, hemp, and lard. They allocated funds for a new Capitol dome. And they ordered weekly mail delivery by land to western settlers between the Mississippi River and San Francisco gold-prospecting camps. Still, the main arguments in Congress were about Kansas and the admission of more slave states.

John C. Breckinridge,
vice-president under
James Buchanan

At 11:00 A.M. on Wednesday, March 4, 1857, Congress adjourned to greet the next president. James Buchanan was the first president who was born in Pennsylvania. He was the only president to remain a bachelor throughout his term. And, at age sixty-five, he was the oldest chief executive yet.

Throngs of well-wishers surrounded the east Capitol porch to see the new president take the oath of office and hear his inaugural address. Buchanan arrived in an open carriage with Vice-President-Elect John Breckinridge of Kentucky and President Pierce. The group was part of a large military parade of magnificent floats carrying model battleships, the Goddess of Liberty, and historic scenes.

Buchanan's inaugural procession down Pennsylvania Avenue in Washington, D.C.

The inaugural ball was a grand affair and the first ever to be photographed. Six thousand people crowded into a specially constructed building that cost taxpayers $15,000. Couples danced to a forty-piece orchestra in a red, white, and blue room under twenty-foot-high ceilings studded with gold stars. Food and drink flowed freely; there were oysters, mutton, venison, tongue, ham, chicken salad, jellies, ice cream, wine, and a four-foot cake.

Harriet, Miss Hetty, and James Buchanan Henry joined President Buchanan for the celebration. Harriet looked brilliant in her white dress decorated with artificial flowers and strands of pearls. Her gaiety easily charmed Washington officials. Beginning with the ball, Harriet served as White House hostess and First Lady for her uncle. She was so popular that reporters dubbed her "Our Democratic Queen."

President Buchanan and his cabinet members

As the party ended, Buchanan was overwhelmed by the enormous task ahead of him. He wrote that "the great object of my administration will be to arrest, if possible, the agitation of slavery to the North, and to destroy sectional parties." Carefully planning to take a middle course, he wondered whether he could meet the challenge.

President Buchanan's first task was to select a cabinet that would represent the interests of the entire nation. There would be no radicals. Instead, Buchanan only chose men who were more devoted to a unified country than to the aims of a given region. His final selection included a balance of southerners and northerners.

Buchanan hoped that his second problem, the slavery issue, would be settled by the Supreme Court decision on the Dred Scott case. Scott was a slave who had lived with

Dred Scott

his master in the free state of Illinois and in the Minnesota and Wisconsin territories before going home to Missouri, a slave state. He sued the government for his freedom, based on his earlier residence on free soil.

The court's final decision to dismiss the case did more than declare that slaves were not citizens under the Constitution. It proclaimed that the Missouri Compromise was null and void and that Congress had no legal power to exclude slaves from the territories. As judges decided the Dred Scott case, proslavery forces in Kansas chose to draft a constitution and apply for statehood. Knowing they were outnumbered by free soilers, Kansas slave owners rigged the vote for a proslavery constitution. In protest, abolitionists boycotted the constitutional convention in Lecompton, Kansas. As a result, it was the proslavery Lecompton constitution that was submitted to Congress.

Outraged free soilers then took over the legislature and called for a vote. This time, slavery advocates boycotted, and the Lecompton constitution was voted down.

Buchanan pressed Congress to admit Kansas under the Lecompton constitution. The Dred Scott decision confirmed his belief that Congress could not interfere with people's right to own property—in this case, slaves. Buchanan understood that the people of Kansas were against slavery. But he figured they could amend the state constitution in their own time. In the meantime, he wanted Kansas admitted as soon as possible to restore peace.

Reactions to this stand were frightening. Debate in Congress led to fist fights between northern and southern members. Republicans denounced the proslavery southern Democrats. Democrat Stephen A. Douglas of Illinois debated bitterly against the president. His attacks further split the Democratic party into proslavery and antislavery forces. Buchanan received support from neither side.

On March 23, 1858, Buchanan strong-armed enough senators into accepting the Lecompton constitution, but it failed in the House. The constitution was sent back to Kansas voters, who then rejected it by a ratio of six to one.

Kansas was finally admitted as a free state, but this did little to calm hostilities between the North and the South. More and more, southerners felt their rights threatened by antislavery groups. Events such as abolitionist John Brown's raid on Harpers Ferry had begun the road to open conflict. After Brown was hanged, northerners honored him as a saint, tolling bells and firing cannons to mark the day of his death. Feelings ran high on both sides.

Above: The arsenal at Harpers Ferry

Right: Democrat Stephen A. Douglas

The slavery issue crippled Buchanan's administration. Congress scrapped many of his domestic and foreign programs as sectional issues. The North vetoed buying Cuba, since it probably would have become another slave state. The South rejected higher tariffs, although this would have expanded the economy.

Still, in spite of opposition, Buchanan made inroads at home and abroad that might have earned him praise during different times.

Relations with Great Britain were on firm ground for the first time in United States history. Buchanan negotiated a peaceful treaty that required Britain to surrender any claims it had on lands within Central America. Britain also gave up its rights to search American ships suspected of carrying slaves.

The president had equal success in the Far East and in Paraguay. With China and Japan, he concluded treaties of commerce. With Paraguay, he peacefully ended that country's hostilities against American seamen. The resulting treaty began commercial and navigation privileges between the two countries. Buchanan's diplomatic skills broadened the rights of American citizens abroad and enhanced the country's reputation worldwide.

At home, parties and social events at the White House reached heights not seen since the days of President Washington. Buchanan, like Washington, dipped into his own savings when entertaining expenses exceeded his $25,000-a-year salary.

Each week Harriet and Buchanan presided over a small dinner party for cabinet members, politicians, and their families. The president had banned dancing and card-playing to satisfy some supporters. Nevertheless, Harriet, with her uncle's agreement, entertained the foremost dignitaries with elegance and style.

Harriet managed the reception for the first Japanese delegation to America. She also entertained the Prince of Wales (later King Edward VII) with a dinner party, an afternoon game of ninepins, and a trip down the Potomac on the steamship U.S.S. *Harriet Lane.*

Harriet carried her role as First Lady beyond hostess. She devoted much of her time to creating a national art gallery and to improving living conditions for American Indians. Because of her concern, many called Harriet the "Great Mother of the Indians." Composer Septimus Winner even dedicated his popular song "Listen to the Mocking Bird" to Harriet. Her popularity, in fact, far exceeded the president's.

All this time, Buchanan knew his political career was ending. Politicians from all sides attacked him as weak or corrupt. Eventually, the Covode Commission totally discredited his administration and left the Democratic party in shambles.

The hopeless split in the Democratic party gave Republicans an edge in the 1860 election. Their platform opposed the expansion of slavery, raising protective tariffs, and increasing federal aid for domestic improvements. Republican candidate Abraham Lincoln easily won the election. Lincoln's support came from free states, an alarming fact to southerners who feared the meddling of abolitionists.

Left: Harriet Lane, Buchanan's niece

Below: A delegation of Pawnee, Ponca, and Potawatomi Indians meeting with President Buchanan at the White House

Above: Buchanan holds a reception for the Prince of Wales at the White House

Right: Buchanan meets with Japanese emissaries

Abraham Lincoln, as photographed by Mathew Brady in 1860

After Lincoln's election, events moved quickly. Panicked southerners moved to withdraw from the Union rather than take a back seat to abolitionists. On December 20, 1860, South Carolinians moved to secede. They believed that withdrawal was the only answer to a Union that ceased to serve the combined interests of all the states. By January 1861, six southern states had followed South Carolina's lead.

Just before secession, President Buchanan's address to Congress blamed northern agitators for sectional problems. While he agreed with the South's right to revolt, he believed the Constitution gave them no right to secede. He

The Confederate attack on Fort Sumter that began the Civil War in April 1861

would maintain federal troops in the southern states, whether they stayed in the Union or not.

After secession, South Carolina forces prepared to seize federal property in the state. In defense, Major Anderson moved all his forces into Fort Sumter in Charleston harbor. This left Fort Moultrie, the post office, and the customs office for local takeover. On January 9, the steamer *Star of the West* approached Charleston harbor to unload supplies for the government forces at Fort Sumter. South Carolinians fired on the ship and it retreated.

A cartoon showing America's condition before and after Buchanan's presidency

President Buchanan refused to send troops to defend Fort Sumter. Western settlers needed their militias to defend themselves against hostile Indians. And Congress denied the president money for more troops. More important, Buchanan did not want to provoke greater hostilities from southerners. His views about slavery and the Constitution prevented him from taking any strong action. Buchanan believed his power to act should come from Congress. Congress, however, had declared war on the administration long ago and refused to make any compromises with the president.

Buchanan portrayed as an "old fashioned gas fixture in the White House"

Because Buchanan could please no side, his cabinet and his ministers quit in droves. The president was left alone to keep the country from active warfare until Lincoln's inauguration. His hope for unity slipped away.

On March 9, 1861, a weary President Buchanan entered a carriage to pick up President-Elect Abraham Lincoln. As the two men rode, Buchanan spoke: "My dear sir, if you are as happy in entering the White House as I shall feel on returning to Wheatland, you are a happy man indeed."

Chapter 8

Retirement without Peace

President Buchanan returned to Lancaster in the same decorated railroad car that had carried him to Washington four years earlier. At the station he was greeted by cheering crowds, ringing church bells, a thirty-four-gun salute, and a parade into town. A band played "Home Sweet Home" as he entered Wheatland.

Initially, Buchanan basked in the warmth of family, friends, and neighbors who visited frequently. Guests often found him wandering the serene grounds of Wheatland. At other times he could be found curled in a comfortable chair reading, with a cigar and a glass of Madeira, and wearing leather slippers and an old dressing gown. Now Buchanan had time for his pet charities, such as the Widow's Fund, which supplied wood to poor widows, and Franklin and Marshall College. People of Lancaster were happy to have their friend "Jimmie" back.

After almost fifty years of public service, Buchanan deserved to retire with honor. But peace for Buchanan *and* the country was short-lived.

On April 12, 1861, the Civil War began when rebel soldiers fired on federal troops in Charleston harbor. To Buchanan's shock, Republicans blamed the war on him. Soon attacks came from all sides.

Buchanan's former cabinet members—including five who had been granted federal jobs by Lincoln—were spreading lies about him. Congress accused James and Harriet of stealing gifts that had been given to the United States by foreign visitors. Buchanan's administration was taken apart piece by piece, and the newspapers broadcast every falsehood.

As the charges intensified, Buchanan began receiving threats. Miss Hetty frequently found notes under the door threatening that fires would be set. The Presbyterian Church refused his membership while the war raged. For safety, Buchanan stopped his trips to Lancaster. Local Masons guarded his home until the war ended.

Attacks became so severe that Buchanan suffered a violent bout of bilious fever. Upon recovery, however, he resolved to write a book in his defense. Buchanan continued to write even when Confederate soldiers advanced to within ten miles of his home. The resulting book was entitled *Mr. Buchanan's Administration on the Eve of the Rebellion.* It was published in 1866, the year after the Civil War ended.

Southern friends wrote to Buchanan about the grief caused by the war. Old northern friends who had lost family members blamed Buchanan. These letters hurt him deeply. So much had happened since he left office that he began to feel his seventy-eight years. Truly, he was the only member still living from the House of Representatives that he had joined in 1821.

In May of 1868, Buchanan took to his bed with a cold and various ailments of old age. Knowing the end was near, Buchanan finalized his will, prepared a simple funeral, and said good-bye to family and friends. The day before he died, Buchanan assured a friend, "I have no regret for any public act of my life, and history will vindicate my memory."

On June 1, 1868, James Buchanan died. His request for a plain ceremony went unnoticed by the more than twenty thousand people who came to remember his "great private virtue, charity, kindness, and courtesy."

To neighbors of Lancaster County, Buchanan would always be their hero. However, the rest of the country was not so kind. In his death notice, the *Springfield Daily Republican* noted that "there was nothing interesting about him. . . . Buchanan was the kind who was not forgiven blunders."

The legacy of slavery overshadowed all Buchanan's good intentions. Detractors held little admiration for his policy of moderation and compromise. Despite a lifetime of public service and outstanding gains in territorial expansion and foreign policy, Buchanan was berated as the man who started the Civil War.

Leaving the issue of the war aside, the Springfield newspaper nevertheless gave him credit for being a peacemaker. James Buchanan, it read, would be remembered as the "president who was willing to concede everything, before he would fight, and then he wouldn't."

The funeral of James Buchanan in Lancaster, Pennsylvania

James Buchanan (1791-1868), fifteenth president of the United States

Chronology of American History

(Shaded area covers events in James Buchanan's lifetime.)

About A.D. 982—Eric the Red, born in Norway, reaches Greenland in one of the first European voyages to North America.

About 1000—Leif Ericson (Eric the Red's son) leads what is thought to be the first European expedition to mainland North America; Leif probably lands in Canada.

1492—Christopher Columbus, seeking a sea route from Spain to the Far East, discovers the New World.

1497—John Cabot reaches Canada in the first English voyage to North America.

1513—Ponce de Léon explores Florida in search of the fabled Fountain of Youth.

1519-1521—Hernando Cortés of Spain conquers Mexico.

1534—French explorers led by Jacques Cartier enter the Gulf of St. Lawrence in Canada.

1540—Spanish explorer Francisco Coronado begins exploring the American Southwest, seeking the riches of the mythical Seven Cities of Cibola.

1565—St. Augustine, Florida, the first permanent European town in what is now the United States, is founded by the Spanish.

1607—Jamestown, Virginia, is founded, the first permanent English town in the present-day U.S.

1608—Frenchman Samuel de Champlain founds the village of Quebec, Canada.

1609—Henry Hudson explores the eastern coast of present-day U.S. for the Netherlands; the Dutch then claim parts of New York, New Jersey, Delaware, and Connecticut and name the area New Netherland.

1619—The English colonies' first shipment of black slaves arrives in Jamestown.

1620—English Pilgrims found Massachusetts' first permanent town at Plymouth.

1621—Massachusetts Pilgrims and Indians hold the famous first Thanksgiving feast in colonial America.

1623—Colonization of New Hampshire is begun by the English.

1624—Colonization of present-day New York State is begun by the Dutch at Fort Orange (Albany).

1625—The Dutch start building New Amsterdam (now New York City).

1630—The town of Boston, Massachusetts, is founded by the English Puritans.

1633—Colonization of Connecticut is begun by the English.

1634—Colonization of Maryland is begun by the English.

1636—Harvard, the colonies' first college, is founded in Massachusetts. Rhode Island colonization begins when Englishman Roger Williams founds Providence.

1638—Delaware colonization begins as Swedes build Fort Christina at present-day Wilmington.

1640—Stephen Daye of Cambridge, Massachusetts, prints *The Bay Psalm Book*, the first English-language book published in what is now the U.S.

1643—Swedish settlers begin colonizing Pennsylvania.

About 1650—North Carolina is colonized by Virginia settlers.

1660—New Jersey colonization is begun by the Dutch at present-day Jersey City.

1670—South Carolina colonization is begun by the English near Charleston.

1673—Jacques Marquette and Louis Jolliet explore the upper Mississippi River for France.

1682—Philadelphia, Pennsylvania, is settled. La Salle explores Mississippi River all the way to its mouth in Louisiana and claims the whole Mississippi Valley for France.

1693—College of William and Mary is founded in Williamsburg, Virginia.

1700—Colonial population is about 250,000.

1703—Benjamin Franklin is born in Boston.

1732—George Washington, first president of the U.S., is born in Westmoreland County, Virginia.

1733—James Oglethorpe founds Savannah, Georgia; Georgia is established as the thirteenth colony.

1735—John Adams, second president of the U.S., is born in Braintree, Massachusetts.

1737—William Byrd founds Richmond, Virginia.

1738—British troops are sent to Georgia over border dispute with Spain.

1739—Black insurrection takes place in South Carolina.

1740—English Parliament passes act allowing naturalization of immigrants to American colonies after seven-year residence.

1743—Thomas Jefferson is born in Albemarle County, Virginia. Benjamin Franklin retires at age thirty-seven to devote himself to scientific inquiries and public service.

1744—King George's War begins; France joins war effort against England.

1745—During King George's War, France raids settlements in Maine and New York.

1747—Classes begin at Princeton College in New Jersey.

1748—The Treaty of Aix-la-Chapelle concludes King George's War.

1749—Parliament legally recognizes slavery in colonies and the inauguration of the plantation system in the South. George Washington becomes the surveyor for Culpepper County in Virginia.

1750—Thomas Walker passes through and names Cumberland Gap on his way toward Kentucky region. Colonial population is about 1,200,000.

1751—James Madison, fourth president of the U.S., is born in Port Conway, Virginia. English Parliament passes Currency Act, banning New England colonies from issuing paper money. George Washington travels to Barbados.

1752—Pennsylvania Hospital, the first general hospital in the colonies, is founded in Philadelphia. Benjamin Franklin uses a kite in a thunderstorm to demonstrate that lightning is a form of electricity.

1753—George Washington delivers command that the French withdraw from the Ohio River Valley; French disregard the demand. Colonial population is about 1,328,000.

1754—French and Indian War begins (extends to Europe as the Seven Years' War). Washington surrenders at Fort Necessity.

1755—French and Indians ambush Braddock. Washington becomes commander of Virginia troops.

1756—England declares war on France.

1758—James Monroe, fifth president of the U.S., is born in Westmoreland County, Virginia.

1759—Cherokee Indian war begins in southern colonies; hostilities extend to 1761. George Washington marries Martha Dandridge Custis.

1760—George III becomes king of England. Colonial population is about 1,600,000.

1762—England declares war on Spain.

1763—Treaty of Paris concludes the French and Indian War and the Seven Years' War. England gains Canada and most other French lands east of the Mississippi River.

1764—British pass the Sugar Act to gain tax money from the colonists. The issue of taxation without representation is first introduced in Boston. John Adams marries Abigail Smith.

1765—Stamp Act goes into effect in the colonies. Business virtually stops as almost all colonists refuse to use the stamps.

1766—British repeal the Stamp Act.

1767—John Quincy Adams, sixth president of the U.S. and son of second president John Adams, is born in Braintree, Massachusetts. Andrew Jackson, seventh president of the U.S., is born in Waxhaw settlement, South Carolina.

1769—Daniel Boone sights the Kentucky Territory.

1770—In the Boston Massacre, British soldiers kill five colonists and injure six. Townshend Acts are repealed, thus eliminating all duties on imports to the colonies except tea.

1771—Benjamin Franklin begins his autobiography, a work that he will never complete. The North Carolina assembly passes the "Bloody Act," which makes rioters guilty of treason.

1772—Samuel Adams rouses colonists to consider British threats to self-government.

1773—English Parliament passes the Tea Act. Colonists dressed as Mohawk Indians board British tea ships and toss 342 casks of tea into the water in what becomes known as the Boston Tea Party. William Henry Harrison is born in Charles City County, Virginia.

1774—British close the port of Boston to punish the city for the Boston Tea Party. First Continental Congress convenes in Philadelphia.

1775—American Revolution begins with battles of Lexington and Concord, Massachusetts. Second Continental Congress opens in Philadelphia. George Washington becomes commander-in-chief of the Continental army.

1776—Declaration of Independence is adopted on July 4.

1777—Congress adopts the American flag with thirteen stars and thirteen stripes. John Adams is sent to France to negotiate peace treaty.

1778—France declares war against Great Britain and becomes U.S. ally.

1779—British surrender to Americans at Vincennes. Thomas Jefferson is elected governor of Virginia. James Madison is elected to the Continental Congress.

1780—Benedict Arnold, first American traitor, defects to the British.

1781—Articles of Confederation go into effect. Cornwallis surrenders to George Washington at Yorktown, ending the American Revolution.

1782—American commissioners, including John Adams, sign peace treaty with British in Paris. Thomas Jefferson's wife, Martha, dies. Martin Van Buren is born in Kinderhook, New York.

1784—Zachary Taylor is born near Barboursville, Virginia.

1785—Congress adopts the dollar as the unit of currency. John Adams is made minister to Great Britain. Thomas Jefferson is appointed minister to France.

1786—Shays's Rebellion begins in Massachusetts.

1787—Constitutional Convention assembles in Philadelphia, with George Washington presiding; U.S. Constitution is adopted. Delaware, New Jersey, and Pennsylvania become states.

1788—Virginia, South Carolina, New York, Connecticut, New Hampshire, Maryland, and Massachusetts become states. U.S. Constitution is ratified. New York City is declared U.S. capital.

1789—Presidential electors elect George Washington and John Adams as first president and vice-president. Thomas Jefferson is appointed secretary of state. North Carolina becomes a state. French Revolution begins.

1790—Supreme Court meets for the first time. Rhode Island becomes a state. First national census in the U.S. counts 3,929,214 persons. John Tyler is born in Charles City County, Virginia.

1791—Vermont enters the Union. U.S. Bill of Rights, the first ten amendments to the Constitution, goes into effect. District of Columbia is established. James Buchanan is born in Stony Batter, Pennsylvania.

1792—Thomas Paine publishes *The Rights of Man*. Kentucky becomes a state. Two political parties are formed in the U.S., Federalist and Republican. Washington is elected to a second term, with Adams as vice-president.

1793—War between France and Britain begins; U.S. declares neutrality. Eli Whitney invents the cotton gin; cotton production and slave labor increase in the South.

1794—Eleventh Amendment to the Constitution is passed, limiting federal courts' power. "Whiskey Rebellion" in Pennsylvania protests federal whiskey tax. James Madison marries Dolley Payne Todd.

1795—George Washington signs the Jay Treaty with Great Britain. Treaty of San Lorenzo, between U.S. and Spain, settles Florida boundary and gives U.S. right to navigate the Mississippi. James Polk is born near Pineville, North Carolina.

1796—Tennessee enters the Union. Washington gives his Farewell Address, refusing a third presidential term. John Adams is elected president and Thomas Jefferson vice-president.

1797—Adams recommends defense measures against possible war with France. Napoleon Bonaparte and his army march against Austrians in Italy. U.S. population is about 4,900,000.

1798—Washington is named commander-in-chief of the U.S. Army. Department of the Navy is created. Alien and Sedition Acts are passed. Napoleon's troops invade Egypt and Switzerland.

1799—George Washington dies at Mount Vernon, New York. James Monroe is elected governor of Virginia. French Revolution ends. Napoleon becomes ruler of France.

1800—Thomas Jefferson and Aaron Burr tie for president. U.S. capital is moved from Philadelphia to Washington, D.C. The White House is built as presidents' home. Spain returns Louisiana to France. Millard Fillmore is born in Locke, New York.

1801—After thirty-six ballots, House of Representatives elects Thomas Jefferson president, making Burr vice-president. James Madison is named secretary of state.

1802—Congress abolishes excise taxes. U.S. Military Academy is founded at West Point, New York.

1803—Ohio enters the Union. Louisiana Purchase treaty is signed with France, greatly expanding U.S. territory.

1804—Twelfth Amendment to the Constitution rules that president and vice-president be elected separately. Alexander Hamilton is killed by Vice-President Aaron Burr in a duel. Orleans Territory is established. Napoleon crowns himself emperor of France. Franklin Pierce is born in Hillsborough Lower Village, New Hampshire.

1805—Thomas Jefferson begins his second term as president. Lewis and Clark expedition reaches the Pacific Ocean.

1806—Coinage of silver dollars is stopped; resumes in 1836.

1807—Aaron Burr is acquitted in treason trial. Embargo Act closes U.S. ports to trade.

1808—James Madison is elected president. Congress outlaws importing slaves from Africa. Andrew Johnson is born in Raleigh, North Carolina.

1809—Abraham Lincoln is born near Hodgenville, Kentucky.

1810—U.S. population is 7,240,000.

1811—William Henry Harrison defeats Indians at Tippecanoe. Monroe is named secretary of state.

1812—Louisiana becomes a state. U.S. declares war on Britain (War of 1812). James Madison is reelected president. Napoleon invades Russia.

1813—British forces take Fort Niagara and Buffalo, New York.

1814—Francis Scott Key writes "The Star-Spangled Banner." British troops burn much of Washington, D.C., including the White House. Treaty of Ghent ends War of 1812. James Monroe becomes secretary of war.

1815—Napoleon meets his final defeat at Battle of Waterloo.

1816—James Monroe is elected president. Indiana becomes a state.

1817—Mississippi becomes a state. Construction on Erie Canal begins.

1818—Illinois enters the Union. The present thirteen-stripe flag is adopted. Border between U.S. and Canada is agreed upon.

1819—Alabama becomes a state. U.S. purchases Florida from Spain. Thomas Jefferson establishes the University of Virginia.

1820—James Monroe is reelected. In the Missouri Compromise, Maine enters the Union as a free (non-slave) state.

1821 — Missouri enters the Union as a slave state. Santa Fe Trail opens the American Southwest. Mexico declares independence from Spain. Napoleon Bonaparte dies.

1822 — U.S. recognizes Mexico and Colombia. Liberia in Africa is founded as a home for freed slaves. Ulysses S. Grant is born in Point Pleasant, Ohio. Rutherford B. Hayes is born in Delaware, Ohio.

1823 — Monroe Doctrine closes North and South America to European colonizing or invasion.

1824 — House of Representatives elects John Quincy Adams president when none of the four candidates wins a majority in national election. Mexico becomes a republic.

1825 — Erie Canal is opened. U.S. population is 11,300,000.

1826 — Thomas Jefferson and John Adams both die on July 4, the fiftieth anniversary of the Declaration of Independence.

1828 — Andrew Jackson is elected president. Tariff of Abominations is passed, cutting imports.

1829 — James Madison attends Virginia's constitutional convention. Slavery is abolished in Mexico. Chester A. Arthur is born in Fairfield, Vermont.

1830 — Indian Removal Act to resettle Indians west of the Mississippi is approved.

1831 — James Monroe dies in New York City. James A. Garfield is born in Orange, Ohio. Cyrus McCormick develops his reaper.

1832 — Andrew Jackson, nominated by the new Democratic Party, is reelected president.

1833 — Britain abolishes slavery in its colonies. Benjamin Harrison is born in North Bend, Ohio.

1835 — Federal government becomes debt-free for the first time.

1836 — Martin Van Buren becomes president. Texas wins independence from Mexico. Arkansas joins the Union. James Madison dies at Montpelier, Virginia.

1837 — Michigan enters the Union. U.S. population is 15,900,000. Grover Cleveland is born in Caldwell, New Jersey.

1840 — William Henry Harrison is elected president.

1841 — President Harrison dies in Washington, D.C., one month after inauguration. Vice-President John Tyler succeeds him.

1843 — William McKinley is born in Niles, Ohio.

1844 — James Knox Polk is elected president. Samuel Morse sends first telegraphic message.

1845 — Texas and Florida become states. Potato famine in Ireland causes massive emigration from Ireland to U.S. Andrew Jackson dies near Nashville, Tennessee.

1846 — Iowa enters the Union. War with Mexico begins.

1847 — U.S. captures Mexico City.

1848 — Zachary Taylor becomes president. Treaty of Guadalupe Hidalgo ends Mexico-U.S. war. Wisconsin becomes a state.

1849 — James Polk dies in Nashville, Tennessee.

1850 — President Taylor dies in Washington, D.C.; Vice-President Millard Fillmore succeeds him. California enters the Union, breaking tie between slave and free states.

1852 — Franklin Pierce is elected president.

1853 — Gadsden Purchase transfers Mexican territory to U.S.

1854 — "War for Bleeding Kansas" is fought between slave and free states.

1855 — Czar Nicholas I of Russia dies, succeeded by Alexander II.

1856 — James Buchanan is elected president. In Massacre of Potawatomi Creek, Kansas-slavers are murdered by free-staters. Woodrow Wilson is born in Staunton, Pennsylvania.

1857 — William Howard Taft is born in Cincinnati, Ohio.

1858 — Minnesota enters the Union. Theodore Roosevelt is born in New York City.

1859 — Oregon becomes a state.

1860—Abraham Lincoln is elected president; South Carolina secedes from the Union in protest.

1861—Arkansas, Tennessee, North Carolina, and Virginia secede. Kansas enters the Union as a free state. Civil War begins.

1862—Union forces capture Fort Henry, Roanoke Island, Fort Donelson, Jacksonville, and New Orleans; Union armies are defeated at the battles of Bull Run and Fredericksburg. Martin Van Buren dies in Kinderhook, New York. John Tyler dies near Charles City, Virginia.

1863—Lincoln issues Emancipation Proclamation: all slaves held in rebelling territories are declared free. West Virginia becomes a state.

1864—Abraham Lincoln is reelected. Nevada becomes a state.

1865—Lincoln is assassinated in Washington, D.C., and succeeded by Andrew Johnson. U.S. Civil War ends on May 26. Thirteenth Amendment abolishes slavery. Warren G. Harding is born in Blooming Grove, Ohio.

1867—Nebraska becomes a state. U.S. buys Alaska from Russia for $7,200,000. Reconstruction Acts are passed.

1868—President Johnson is impeached for violating Tenure of Office Act, but is acquitted by Senate. Ulysses S. Grant is elected president. Fourteenth Amendment prohibits voting discrimination. James Buchanan dies in Lancaster, Pennsylvania.

1869—Franklin Pierce dies in Concord, New Hampshire.

1870—Fifteenth Amendment gives blacks the right to vote.

1872—Grant is reelected over Horace Greeley. General Amnesty Act pardons ex-Confederates. Calvin Coolidge is born in Plymouth Notch, Vermont.

1874—Millard Fillmore dies in Buffalo, New York. Herbert Hoover is born in West Branch, Iowa.

1875—Andrew Johnson dies in Carter's Station, Tennessee.

1876—Colorado enters the Union. "Custer's last stand": he and his men are massacred by Sioux Indians at Little Big Horn, Montana.

1877—Rutherford B. Hayes is elected president as all disputed votes are awarded to him.

1880—James A. Garfield is elected president.

1881—President Garfield is assassinated and dies in Elberon, New Jersey. Vice-President Chester A. Arthur succeeds him.

1882—U.S. bans Chinese immigration. Franklin D. Roosevelt is born in Hyde Park, New York.

1885—Ulysses S. Grant dies in Mount McGregor, New York.

1886—Statue of Liberty is dedicated. Chester A. Arthur dies in New York City.

1888—Benjamin Harrison is elected president.

1889—North Dakota, South Dakota, Washington, and Montana become states.

1890—Dwight D. Eisenhower is born in Denison, Texas. Idaho and Wyoming become states.

1892—Grover Cleveland is elected president.

1893—Rutherford B. Hayes dies in Fremont, Ohio.

1896—William McKinley is elected president. Utah becomes a state.

1898—U.S. declares war on Spain over Cuba.

1899—Philippines demand independence from U.S.

1900—McKinley is reelected. Boxer Rebellion against foreigners in China begins.

1901—McKinley is assassinated by anarchist Leon Czolgosz in Buffalo, New York; Theodore Roosevelt becomes president. Benjamin Harrison dies in Indianapolis, Indiana.

1902—U.S. acquires perpetual control over Panama Canal.

1903—Alaskan frontier is settled.

1904—Russian-Japanese War breaks out. Theodore Roosevelt wins presidential election.

1905—Treaty of Portsmouth signed, ending Russian-Japanese War.

1906—U.S. troops occupy Cuba.

1907—President Roosevelt bars all Japanese immigration. Oklahoma enters the Union.

1908—William Howard Taft becomes president. Grover Cleveland dies in Princeton, New Jersey. Lyndon B. Johnson is born near Stonewall, Texas.

1909—NAACP is founded under W.E.B. DuBois

1910—China abolishes slavery.

1911—Chinese Revolution begins. Ronald Reagan is born in Tampico, Illinois.

1912—Woodrow Wilson is elected president. Arizona and New Mexico become states.

1913—Federal income tax is introduced in U.S. through the Sixteenth Amendment. Richard Nixon is born in Yorba Linda, California. Gerald Ford is born in Omaha, Nebraska.

1914—World War I begins.

1915—British liner *Lusitania* is sunk by German submarine.

1916—Wilson is reelected president.

1917—U.S. breaks diplomatic relations with Germany. Czar Nicholas of Russia abdicates as revolution begins. U.S. declares war on Austria-Hungary. John F. Kennedy is born in Brookline, Massachusetts.

1918—Wilson proclaims "Fourteen Points" as war aims. On November 11, armistice is signed between Allies and Germany.

1919—Eighteenth Amendment prohibits sale and manufacture of intoxicating liquors. Wilson presides over first League of Nations; wins Nobel Peace Prize. Theodore Roosevelt dies in Oyster Bay, New York.

1920—Nineteenth Amendment (women's suffrage) is passed. Warren Harding is elected president.

1921—Adolf Hitler's stormtroopers begin to terrorize political opponents.

1922—Irish Free State is established. Soviet states form USSR. Benito Mussolini forms Fascist government in Italy.

1923—President Harding dies in San Francisco, California; he is succeeded by Vice-President Calvin Coolidge.

1924—Coolidge is elected president. Woodrow Wilson dies in Washington, D.C. James Carter is born in Plains, Georgia.

1925—Hitler reorganizes Nazi Party and publishes first volume of *Mein Kampf*.

1926—Fascist youth organizations founded in Germany and Italy. Republic of Lebanon proclaimed.

1927—Stalin becomes Soviet dictator. Economic conference in Geneva attended by fifty-two nations.

1928—Herbert Hoover is elected president. U.S. and many other nations sign Kellogg-Briand pacts to outlaw war.

1929—Stock prices in New York crash on "Black Thursday"; the Great Depression begins.

1930—Bank of U.S. and its many branches close (most significant bank failure of the year). William Howard Taft dies in Washington, D.C.

1931—Emigration from U.S. exceeds immigration for first time as Depression deepens.

1932—Franklin D. Roosevelt wins presidential election in a Democratic landslide.

1933—First concentration camps are erected in Germany. U.S. recognizes USSR and resumes trade. Twenty-First Amendment repeals prohibition. Calvin Coolidge dies in Northampton, Massachusetts.

1934—Severe dust storms hit Plains states. President Roosevelt passes U.S. Social Security Act.

1936—Roosevelt is reelected. Spanish Civil War begins. Hitler and Mussolini form Rome-Berlin Axis.

1937—Roosevelt signs Neutrality Act.

1938—Roosevelt sends appeal to Hitler and Mussolini to settle European problems amicably.

1939—Germany takes over Czechoslovakia and invades Poland, starting World War II.

1940—Roosevelt is reelected for a third term.

1941—Japan bombs Pearl Harbor, U.S. declares war on Japan. Germany and Italy declare war on U.S.; U.S. then declares war on them.

1942—Allies agree not to make separate peace treaties with the enemies. U.S. government transfers more than 100,000 Nisei (Japanese-Americans) from west coast to inland concentration camps.

1943—Allied bombings of Germany begin.

1944—Roosevelt is reelected for a fourth term. Allied forces invade Normandy on D-Day.

1945—President Franklin D. Roosevelt dies in Warm Springs, Georgia; Vice-President Harry S. Truman succeeds him. Mussolini is killed; Hitler commits suicide. Germany surrenders. U.S. drops atomic bomb on Hiroshima; Japan surrenders: end of World War II.

1946—U.N. General Assembly holds its first session in London. Peace conference of twenty-one nations is held in Paris.

1947—Peace treaties are signed in Paris. "Cold War" is in full swing.

1948—U.S. passes Marshall Plan Act, providing $17 billion in aid for Europe. U.S. recognizes new nation of Israel. India and Pakistan become free of British rule. Truman is elected president.

1949—Republic of Eire is proclaimed in Dublin. Russia blocks land route access from Western Germany to Berlin; airlift begins. U.S., France, and Britain agree to merge their zones of occupation in West Germany. Apartheid program begins in South Africa.

1950—Riots in Johannesburg, South Africa, against apartheid. North Korea invades South Korea. U.N. forces land in South Korea and recapture Seoul.

1951—Twenty-Second Amendment limits president to two terms.

1952—Dwight D. Eisenhower resigns as supreme commander in Europe and is elected president.

1953—Stalin dies; struggle for power in Russia follows. Rosenbergs are executed for espionage.

1954—U.S. and Japan sign mutual defense agreement.

1955—Blacks in Montgomery, Alabama, boycott segregated bus lines.

1956—Eisenhower is reelected president. Soviet troops march into Hungary.

1957—U.S. agrees to withdraw ground forces from Japan. Russia launches first satellite, *Sputnik*.

1958—European Common Market comes into being. Alaska becomes the forty-ninth state. Fidel Castro begins war against Batista government in Cuba.

1959—Hawaii becomes fiftieth state. Castro becomes premier of Cuba. De Gaulle is proclaimed president of the Fifth Republic of France.

1960—Historic debates between Senator John F. Kennedy and Vice-President Richard Nixon are televised. Kennedy is elected president. Brezhnev becomes president of USSR.

1961—Berlin Wall is constructed. Kennedy and Khrushchev confer in Vienna. In Bay of Pigs incident, Cubans trained by CIA attempt to overthrow Castro.

1962—U.S. military council is established in South Vietnam.

1963—Riots and beatings by police and whites mark civil rights demonstrations in Birmingham, Alabama; 30,000 troops are called out, Martin Luther King, Jr., is arrested. Freedom marchers descend on Washington, D.C., to demonstrate. President Kennedy is assassinated in Dallas, Texas; Vice-President Lyndon B. Johnson is sworn in as president.

1964—U.S. aircraft bomb North Vietnam. Johnson is elected president. Herbert Hoover dies in New York City.

1965—U.S. combat troops arrive in South Vietnam.

1966—Thousands protest U.S. policy in Vietnam. National Guard quells race riots in Chicago.

1967—Six-Day War between Israel and Arab nations.

1968—Martin Luther King, Jr., is assassinated in Memphis, Tennessee. Senator Robert Kennedy is assassinated in Los Angeles. Riots and police brutality take place at Democratic National Convention in Chicago. Richard Nixon is elected president. Czechoslovakia is invaded by Soviet troops.

1969—Dwight D. Eisenhower dies in Washington, D.C. Hundreds of thousands of people in several U.S. cities demonstrate against Vietnam War.

1970—Four Vietnam War protesters are killed by National Guardsmen at Kent State University in Ohio.

1971—Twenty-Sixth Amendment allows eighteen-year-olds to vote.

1972—Nixon visits Communist China; is reelected president in near-record landslide. Watergate affair begins when five men are arrested in the Watergate hotel complex in Washington, D.C. Nixon announces resignations of aides Haldeman, Ehrlichman, and Dean and Attorney General Kleindienst as a result of Watergate-related charges. Harry S. Truman dies in Kansas City, Missouri.

1973—Vice-President Spiro Agnew resigns; Gerald Ford is named vice-president. Vietnam peace treaty is formally approved after nineteen months of negotiations. Lyndon B. Johnson dies in San Antonio, Texas.

1974—As a result of Watergate cover-up, impeachment is considered; Nixon resigns and Ford becomes president. Ford pardons Nixon and grants limited amnesty to Vietnam War draft evaders and military deserters.

1975—U.S. civilians are evacuated from Saigon, South Vietnam, as Communist forces complete takeover of South Vietnam.

1976—U.S. celebrates its Bicentennial. James Earl Carter becomes president.

1977—Carter pardons most Vietnam draft evaders, numbering some 10,000.

1980—Ronald Reagan is elected president.

1981—President Reagan is shot in the chest in assassination attempt. Sandra Day O'Connor is appointed first woman justice of the Supreme Court.

1983—U.S. troops invade island of Grenada.

1984—Reagan is reelected president. Democratic candidate Walter Mondale's running mate, Geraldine Ferraro, is the first woman selected for vice-president by a major U.S. political party.

1985—Soviet Communist Party secretary Konstantin Chernenko dies; Mikhail Gorbachev succeeds him. U.S. and Soviet officials discuss arms control in Geneva. Reagan and Gorbachev hold summit conference in Geneva. Racial tensions accelerate in South Africa.

1986—Space shuttle *Challenger* explodes shortly after takeoff; crew of seven dies. U.S. bombs bases in Libya. Corazon Aquino defeats Ferdinand Marcos in Philippine presidential election.

1987—Iraqi missile rips the U.S. frigate *Stark* in the Persian Gulf, killing thirty-seven American sailors. Congress holds hearings to investigate sale of U.S. arms to Iran to finance Nicaraguan *contra* movement.

Index

Page numbers in boldface type indicate illustrations.

About the Author

Marlene Targ Brill is a free-lance Chicago-area writer, specializing in fiction and nonfiction books, articles, media, and other educational materials for children. Among her credits are biographical contributions to *World Book Encyclopedia's The President's World* and social studies and science articles for *Encyclopaedia Britannica*. Ms. Brill holds a B.A. in Special Education from the University of Illinois and an M.A. in Early Childhood Education from Roosevelt University. She currently writes for health care, business, and young people's publications, and is active in Chicago Women in Publishing and Independent Writers of Chicago.